DISCARD

WEST GEORGIA REGIONAL LIBRARY SYSTEM
Neva Lomason Memorial Library

America, My Country
Native Peoples

The Pawnee

By Heather N. Kolich

Content Review, With Special Thanks
Marshall Gover
Pawnee
President, Pawnee Business Council
Pawnee Nation of Oklahoma
Pawnee, Oklahoma

Your State • Your Standards • Your Grade Level

Dear Educators, Librarians and Parents . . .

Thank you for choosing books from State Standards Publishing! This book supports state Departments of Educations' standards for elementary level social studies and has been measured by the ATOS Readability Formula for Books (Accelerated Reader), the Lexile Framework for Reading, and the Fountas & Pinnell Benchmark Assessment System for Guided Reading. Photographs and/or illustrations, captions, and other design elements have been included to provide supportive visual messaging to enhance text comprehension. Glossary and Word Index sections introduce key new words and help young readers develop skills in locating and combining information. "Think With Bagster" questions provide teachers and parents with tools for additional learning activities and critical thinking development. We wish you all success in using this book to meet your student or child's learning needs.

Jill Ward, President

Publisher

State Standards Publishing, LLC
1788 Quail Hollow
Hamilton, GA 31811, USA
1.866.740.3056, www.statestandardspublishing.com

Cataloging-in-Publication Data

Kolich, Heather N.
   The Pawnee / Heather N. Kolich.
     p. cm. -- (America, my country Native Peoples)
   Includes index.
   ISBN 978-1-935884-92-7 (lib. bdg.)
   ISBN 978-1-935884-98-9 (pbk.)
   1. Pawnee Indians--Juvenile literature.   I. Title.
   978.004--dc23

                          2012948401

Copyright © 2013 by State Standards Publishing, LLC. All rights reserved. No part of this book may be reproduced, stored, or transmitted in any form or by any means without prior written permission from the publisher. Printed in the United States of America, North Mankato, Minnesota, August 2012, 060512.

About the Author

Heather N. Kolich has a Bachelor of Science degree in animal science from the University of Georgia. She works with Forsyth County Cooperative Extension in agriculture and natural resources. She has also been a freelance writer for 13 years and has numerous published articles for children and adults. Heather enjoys learning new things and sharing knowledge with others. She also likes to grow and can her own food.

Editor's Note:

The Pawnee population figures stated on page 26 have been documented from both recognized reference and governmental primary sources. The Pawnee Nation believes these numbers to be higher, with populations of 40,000 to 50,000 in the year 1800, and 12,000 to 15,000 in the year 1875.

1 2 3 4 5 – CG – 17 16 15 14 13

Table of Contents

A Long Migration 5

Endless Views 6

The Creation Story 9

Village Homes 10

Social Order 13

Farming and Gathering 14

Weapons and War 17

The Bison Hunt 18

Games, Crafts, Clothing, and Trade 21

Gold, Fur, and Horses 22

The Push West 25

Pawnees Lessen 26

Pawnees Today 29

Glossary 30

Index 31

Think With Bagster 32

Hi, I'm Bagster! Let's learn about Native Peoples.

The Pawnees lived along the Platte and other rivers in Nebraska and Kansas.

A Long Migration

The four **bands** of the Pawnee Indians lived, farmed, and hunted on the Great Plains of North America. They were one of the Native American tribes known as Plains Indians and are probably the oldest Plains tribe. The Skidi (skee-dee) "Wolf" band may have settled along the Republican River before 1300 A.D. This river runs through what is now northern Kansas and southern Nebraska. This band had villages farther north, near the Loup River in central Nebraska, by 1400 A.D. The other three Pawnee bands built settlements along the Platte River and the Republican River. They are the Chaui (chau-wee) "Grand," the Kitkehahki (kit-kuh-hah-kee) "Republican," and the Pitahawirata "Tappage" (pit-ah-wih-rah-tah top-pidge) bands. The Platte River runs between the Republican and Loup rivers.

Pawnees spoke a Caddoan language, like the Caddo Indians who lived nearby. But Pawnees believed they **migrated** up from Central America into the Southwest. It took hundreds of years for them to migrate to Kansas and Nebraska. Those who did became known as the Pawnees.

According to Pawnee oral tradition, the Pawnee may be related to the Aztecs from Central America. They may have migrated from as far as Mexico into present-day Texas.

Endless Views

On the Great Plains, the sky seems to arc overhead like a huge dome. Tall, waving grasses flow in every direction. No forests or mountains break the wind. For the migrating Pawnees, only herds of bison broke the long view of the Great Plains.

In ancient times, animals called mammoths and mastodons grazed on the grasses of the Great Plains. When the Pawnees arrived, millions of bison, or buffalo, roamed the vast, rolling **prairies**. Lakes dotted the land. Thin strips of trees lined the banks of fish-filled rivers.

The grass made the land look flat, but it was full of swells and dips. Antelope, elk, and deer grazed among low, rolling hills. Jackrabbits, game birds, and wolves hid in the many different grasses. Other wild plants grew on the prairie, too. The soil was rich.

Prairie weather changed quickly. A sunny day could become stormy in minutes. Dangerous snow storms, or blizzards, struck with very little warning. Tornados and hail ripped across the prairie. A month might pass with no rain. But the wind always blew.

Animals, plants, soil, and rivers provided the Pawnees with everything they needed to live. These **natural resources** encouraged them to settle on the Great Plains. They liked the wide space and the star-filled sky.

For the migrating Pawnees, only herds of bison broke the long view of the Great Plains.

What do these pictures tell you about the Pawnee way of life?

When the Pawnees arrived, millions of bison roamed the vast prairies.

Religious ceremonies were connected to sacred bundles like this.

Pawnees believed that Atius Tirawahut made the universe. Atius means "the Father." Tirawahut means "the Universe" and "Father of Everything."

The Creation Story

Pawnees believed that Atius Tirawahut (ah-tee-us tee-rah-wah-huht) made the universe with his thoughts. Atias's first creation was Evening Star. He placed her in the western sky. The moon was her helper. Next, Atius placed Morning Star in the eastern sky. The sun was his helper. Then Atius created North Star and South Star. These stars held up the heavens.

Evening Star made the earth with lightning and thunder. She married Morning Star. They had a daughter who went to live on earth. Their second child, First Man, went to earth, too. Evening Star taught women how to build homes and care for the earth. Morning Star taught men how to hunt and protect their families.

First Man built a village in the middle of all the people. He called it Center Village. He asked people of the other villages to come to Center Village for a meeting. First Man gave each village a bison hide package filled with sacred items, like tools and **regalia** for a ceremony and a perfect ear of corn. Religious ceremonies were connected to these **sacred bundles**. The village or person who owned a particular sacred bundle could direct the ceremony it represented.

Morning Star and Evening Star were not actually stars. Morning Star was Mars and Evening Star was Venus. These two planets were very bright in the sky at the beginning and end of the day.

Village Homes

Pawnees had tent-like travel homes for hunting, called **tipis**. They had a fixed home for farming. When it was time to plant seeds and harvest crops, the bands lived in villages. Their homes were large domes made of timber, mud, stones, and grass. Several to hundreds of these **earth lodges** made up a village. Pawnees also built **sweat lodges**. These were used for a purification, or cleansing, ceremony or to purify the body for other ceremonies. They also prepared for ceremonies with a steam bath. The lodges in each village were positioned to copy a pattern of stars in the night sky.

Women built and owned the circular earth lodges. Four sturdy cottonwood timbers held up the roof, like the four stars that held up the heavens. The roof was shaped in an arc, like the sky. A long entryway stuck out on the east side. A raised altar on the west side held the sacred bundle, which was hung above the altar. A bison skull sat on the altar, below the bundle. As many as 50 people slept in beds against the walls. A fire inside the lodge was used for cooking and keeping warm. The roof had an opening in the center to let smoke from the fire escape.

The earth lodge was a large dome made of timber, mud, stones, and grass.

Pawnees had tent-like travel homes for hunting, called tipis.

Pawnee bands lived in villages of earth lodges.

Women collected water from streams in pottery that they crafted.

Men had political, religious, and healing duties. Some, like the kurahu, watched the stars for signs.

12

Social Order

A yearly cycle of religious observances gave order to the Pawnee people's lives. Work kept them busy, too. Women made almost everything the tribe used. They collected water from streams and cooked meals in clay pottery that they crafted. They wove prairie grasses into mats for lodges and baskets for gathering food. They made boats and tipis from bison hides. They wove fishing nets from willow branches or strips of hide. They sewed clothing. They made tools. They raised children, but grandparents often helped with this task.

Pawnees were honored to do work that helped the whole tribe. Cooking for everyone in the earth lodge was a big task. Women on the north side of the lodge worked together to cook the morning meal. The women on the south side cooked the evening meal.

Men had political, religious, and healing duties. Each village had a leader called a **nasharo** (nah-shah-row). The people respected him and valued his advice. A healer, or **kuraa'u'** (koo-rah-oo), called on the spirits of earthly things, like animals and birds, to heal illnesses. Priests, or **kurahu** (koo-rah-hoo), watched the stars for signs. Events in the heavens told the kurahu when to have religious ceremonies, when to plant crops, and when to leave the village for hunting.

Farming and Gathering

Pawnee women were skilled farmers. They played a major role in the Corn Planting Ceremony. In this spring ceremony, Pawnees asked Atius Tirawahut to protect their crops. Every winter, Atius chose a woman in each village to dream about the Corn Planting Ceremony. She told the kurahu what she saw in her vision. Then, she had the honor of preparing bison meat for the ceremony. She also danced the day before the event. At the Corn Planting Ceremony, holy men dug into the field with four sacred hoes made from bison shoulder blades. Then everyone helped plant corn.

Prairie grass and soil was too tough and dense for farming. Pawnee women cleared land beside rivers that flooded. They planted corn, squash, beans, melons, and tobacco in these fields. Corn and beans grew together. Bean vines climbed up the sturdy corn stalks.

Women also gathered wild foods from the prairie. They collected prairie turnips, chokecherries, persimmons, prickly pear fruit, and peas. They dug pits to store their harvest. All of these things were gifts from Atius. Pawnees gave thanks when they took natural resources from the earth.

Pawnee women owned the harvest. They traded extra food with other people or tribes.

16 Pawnee warriors defended their villages from other Plains tribes.

Weapons and War

Men made spears, clubs, bison skin shields, and bows for hunting and for war. They made sharp arrows with **flint** points. They had to defend their villages from other Plains tribes. Pawnee warriors removed most of their clothing before a battle. Arrows and bullets punched clothing into wounds. This could lead to **infection**, or sickness caused by germs. Infection could kill a warrior long after the battle ended.

Pawnee men respected their enemies. They showed bravery by sneaking up to touch a living enemy. This act of daring was called a **coup** (koo). Stealing an enemy's horse was another type of coup. Coups helped warriors gain standing in the tribe. They kept track of their daring by counting coup.

Fire was another important weapon. Pawnee men burned the grass in areas of the prairie. This took hiding places away from enemy warriors.

Fire was an important weapon, but it was also a useful tool. Burning the prairie removed old grass so that new, tender grass could grow. It encouraged bison herds to move to grazing grounds where they would be easier to hunt.

17

The Bison Hunt

In June and November, Pawnees left their villages for several months to hunt bison. A good bison hunt provided months of meat and fat for the whole tribe. Pawnee women packed traveling supplies and tipis onto a kind of sled pulled by village dogs. This sled, called a **travois** (trah-voy), was made of two long poles that dragged on the ground. A shelf or basket attached between the poles held them apart behind the dog's tail.

Pawnee and other Plains Indians hunted on foot, and later, on horses. Pawnee scouts traveled ahead of the group to look for bison. When they found a herd, hunt police made sure everyone stayed quiet. Then the hunters frightened the herd to make the bison run, or **stampede**. Bison ran over each other. Hunters killed the hurt animals. Sometimes, they chased herds over cliffs. Most bison died from the fall. After the hunt, Pawnee women cut thin strips of meat and hung them in the wind to dry. They preserved hides. They cleaned bones and horns for tools. Pawnees used every part of the animals they killed. They would not waste gifts from Atius.

Pawnee scouts wore wolf skins when searching for bison. Bison ran from men, but they did not fear wolves.

The travois was made of two long poles that dragged on the ground.

Hunters frightened the herd to make the bison stampede.

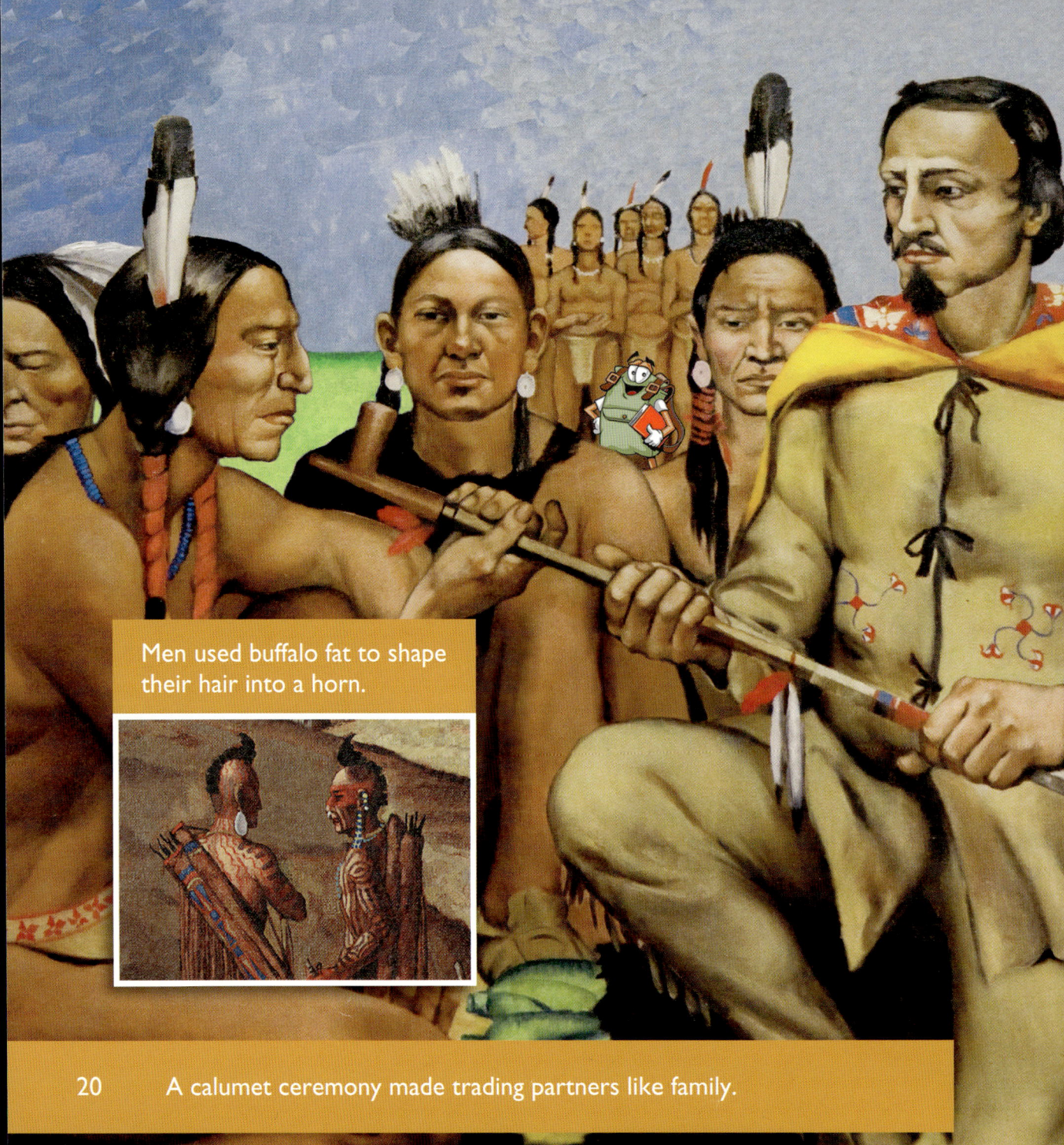

Men used buffalo fat to shape their hair into a horn.

20 A calumet ceremony made trading partners like family.

Games, Crafts, Clothing, and Trade

Pawnees worked hard, but they played, too. Adults had social clubs for planning ceremonies, telling stories, and making crafts. They also played dice games and sports. Men threw spears through rolling hoops. Boys played hunting and war games. Girls had dolls and toy tipis.

The Pawnee used porcupine quills and paints to make patterns and pictures on their clothes. These decorations showed a person's rank. Women wore deerskin skirts and shirts. Men wore leg coverings called leggings and a **breechcloth** with a belt. A second belt held tools. They used buffalo fat to shape their hair into a horn. Everyone wore moccasins for shoes. In winter, men added shirts and women added leggings. They wrapped up in robes made from bison hides. Pictures on the robes told stories of battles and hunts.

Pawnees traded hides, pottery, food, and other goods with tribes who spoke different languages. Plains Indians developed a special sign language to communicate with each other. French and English fur traders learned this sign language, too. A calumet (kal-you-met) ceremony made the trading partners like family. The **calumet** was a pipe that the trading partners smoked together. Through this ceremony, Pawnees could trade with enemy tribes.

The pipe ceremony, called calumet by many tribes, was a way of expressing blessing and respect among people. The pipe was always passed stem first with both hands to symbolize this blessing. For the Pawnee, the smoke represented the breath of Atius.

Gold, Fur, and Horses

In 1541, an explorer named Francisco Vasquez de Coronado led Spanish soldiers into the Great Plains. They rode on horseback, searching for gold. They found none, but their travels brought horses to the Plains. In 1680, Hopi and other Pueblo Indian tribes in New Mexico fought the Spaniards and beat them. The Hopi had learned that horses made hunting and traveling easier. They traded Spanish horses to other tribes. Soon, the Pawnee and other Plains Indians began hunting and traveling on horseback.

French fur traders made friends with Plains Indian tribes in the early 1700s. France made peace agreements, or **treaties**, between the French government and several Plains tribes, including the Pawnee and Oto. The traders gave the Indians guns and metal tools in exchange for bison hides and beaver furs.

Spain and France were at war. Both nations claimed to own the Great Plains. Spain sent Pedro de Villasur and a small army to Nebraska in 1720. Villasur's job was to capture French fur traders. A group of Pawnee and Oto warriors fought the Spaniards and beat them again. Spain gave up and left the land to the traders and the Plains Indians.

In the late 1700s, British companies from England built trading posts in the Great Plains. Indians caught diseases from the white traders. Smallpox and measles killed thousands of Plains Indians.

Soon the Pawnee and other Plains Indians began hunting and traveling on horseback.

How do you think Spanish explorers changed the Pawnee way of life?

Coronado led Spanish explorers into the Great Plains on horseback.

Many Plains Indians wanted to keep white settlers out of their lands.

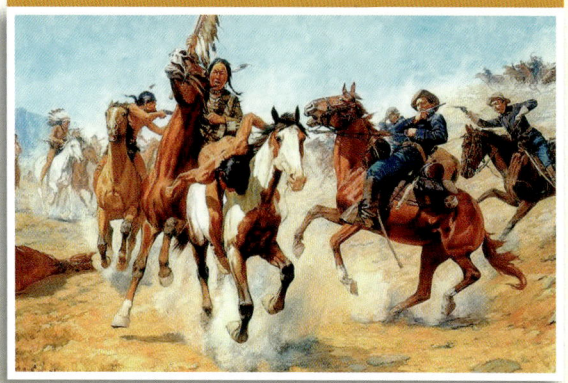

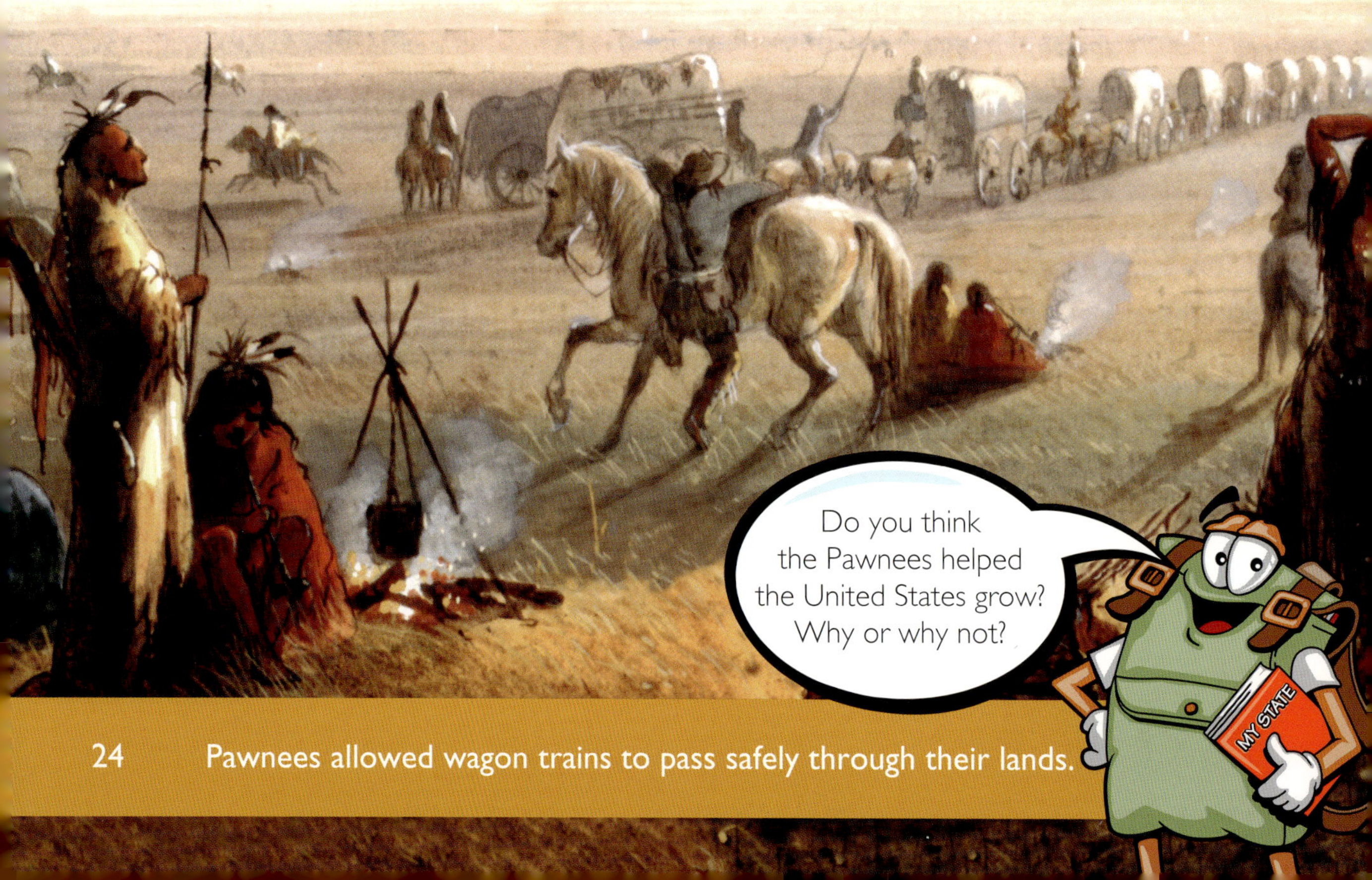
Do you think the Pawnees helped the United States grow? Why or why not?
MY STATE

Pawnees allowed wagon trains to pass safely through their lands.

The Push West

In 1803, the United States bought 828,000 square miles of land from France. The **Louisiana Purchase** doubled the size of the United States. Much of the Great Plains became U.S. property in that deal. With government encouragement, brave Americans headed west. They drove covered wagons across the Great Plains on their way to present-day Oregon and California. Pawnees allowed wagon trains to pass safely through their lands.

Wagon travel was hard, dangerous, and slow. The government decided to build a railroad track all the way to California. This was the **Transcontinental Railroad**. It ran through Pawnee lands.

Many other Plains Indians wanted to keep white settlers out of their lands. They attacked wagons, settlers, and railroad workers. The U.S. Army fought these tribes. Pawnee warriors worked as scouts for the Army during wars with their old enemies, the Sioux and Cheyenne. The Army also hired Pawnees to keep railroad workers and supplies safe from unfriendly tribes.

It took six years to complete the Transcontinental Railroad track. Some railroad crews laid track east from California. Others laid track west from Nebraska, where track from the east coast stopped. The two railroad lines met at Promontory Summit in Utah in 1869. They were joined together with a golden spike.

Pawnees Lessen

The Transcontinental Railroad was bad for Plains Indians. It brought thousands of settlers into their lands. Towns sprang up along the railroad line. People built farms and fences. Bison could not roam freely over the prairies anymore. Other people hunted bison. Settlers and travelers shot bison and elk from train windows and tracks. Sport hunters took the tongues and hides, but left the meat to rot on the prairie. By the end of the 1860s, there were hardly any bison left.

The Pawnee population lessened, too. Around 1800, about 10,000 or more Pawnees lived in Nebraska and Kansas. In 1833 and 1857, Pawnees signed treaties with the United States government. They gave up their hunting territory and weapons. In return, the U.S. gave them money, supplies, and land called a **reservation**. The Pawnees would farm, and the government would protect them. Sioux warriors attacked the Pawnee reservation regularly. The U.S. government was not there to help. By 1875, the 2,000 remaining Pawnees moved to another reservation in Oklahoma. Conditions there were poor. By 1901, only a little over 600 Pawnees were still alive.

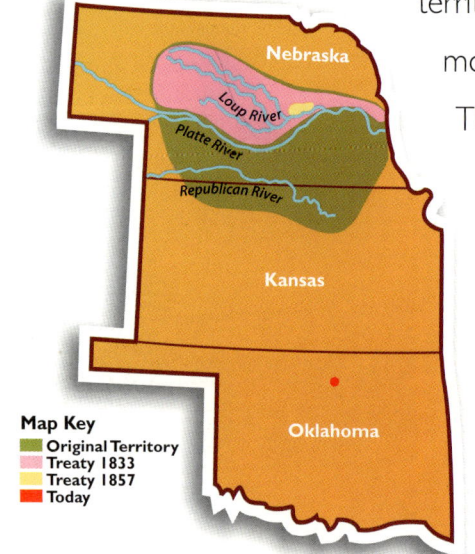

Towns sprang up along the railroad line.

Settlers and travelers shot bison and elk from train windows and tracks.

27

Indian Affairs

Pawnee Nation Flag

Military Service

Pawnees Today

On the reservation in northeast Oklahoma, the U.S. government worked very hard to force Pawnees to adopt white culture. Instead of traditional nasharo leaders, U.S. government agents guided the Pawnee bands. Rather than living together in earth lodges in villages, families lived in houses on separate farms. Men were expected to farm, but women were not.

Life in Oklahoma was very hard for Pawnees. Poverty, unemployment, and depression are still problems on the reservation. But Pawnees stayed loyal to the United States. Pawnee tribe members have served in all branches of the U. S. military. These soldiers have defended the U.S. in eight wars. The flag of the Pawnee Nation bears an arrowhead for each war.

Today, the Pawnee Nation has over 3,200 members. Many live on or near the Pawnee reservation in Pawnee County, Oklahoma. Others, especially the soldiers, found opportunities in the wider world. In 2005, the Pawnee Nation of Oklahoma opened the Pawnee Nation College. The school is open to native and non-native students. Students can earn high school and college credit, or train for skilled jobs. Pawnees live and work in several U.S. states and in other countries. Two members of the Pawnee Nation, Kevin Gover and Larry EchoHawk, served our country as Assistant Secretary of the Interior for Indian Affairs.

Glossary

band – A group of people who inhabit common territory, often based on kinship.

breechcloth – Cloth or animal skin hung from the waist and attached with a belt. Also called a loincloth.

calumet – A pipe smoked as part of a ceremony. Sometimes called a peace pipe.

coup – An act of daring that showed bravery.

earth lodge – A permanent, dome-shaped home made of timber, mud, stones, and grass.

flint – A type of stone that can be shaped into sharp arrowheads and spear points.

infection – Sickness caused by germs.

kuraa'u' – A Pawnee doctor, or healer.

kurahu – A Pawnee priest.

Louisiana Purchase – A vast land purchase that extended the borders of United States territory from the Mississippi River to the Rocky Mountains and from the Gulf of Mexico to Canada.

migrate – To move from one country or region to another.

nasharo – A Pawnee village leader.

natural resources – Things that come directly from nature that are useful to humans.

prairie – A large area of level or rolling grassland.

regalia – Special clothing and ornaments worn for ceremonies and special occasions.

reservation – An area of land set aside by the U.S. government for the use of American Indians.

sacred bundle – A bison hide package filled with sacred items.

stampede – A wild rush or flight of frightened animals.

sweat lodge – A steam bath building where Pawnee Indians bathed or purified their bodies.

tipi – A cone-shaped tent used by American Indians as a home, usually made from animal skins or woven grasses.

Transcontinental Railroad – A track that connected the east and west coasts of Amercia.

travois – A type of sled mounted to an animal and used to carry goods.

treaty – A formal agreement between two or more countries or groups.

Index

animal, 6, 13, 18
Atias Tirawa Hut, 9, 14, 18, 21
band, 5, 10, 29
bison, 6, 9, 10, 13, 14, 17, 18, 21, 22, 26
breechcloth, 21
calumet, 21
ceremony, 9, 10, 13, 14, 21
clothes, clothing, 13, 17, 21
corn, 9, 14
coup, 17
crop, 10, 13, 14
disease, 22
earth, earth lodge, 9, 10, 13, 14, 29
explorer, 22
family, 9, 10, 21, 29
farm, farming, 5, 10, 14, 26, 29
fire, 10, 17
fish, fishing, 6, 13
flint, 17
food, 13, 14, 21
France, French, 21, 22, 25
government, 22, 25, 26, 29
grass, 6, 10, 13, 14, 17
Great Plains, 5, 6, 17, 18, 21, 22, 25, 26

heavens, 9, 10, 13
hide, 13, 18, 21, 22, 26
horse, 17, 18, 22
hunt, hunting, 5, 9, 10, 13, 17, 18, 21, 22, 26
Kansas, 5, 26
kuraa'u, kurahu, 13, 14
land, 6, 14, 22, 25, 26
Louisiana Purchase, 25
man, men, 9, 13, 14, 17, 18, 21, 29
meat, 14, 18, 26
migrated, migrating, 5, 6
nasharo, 13, 29
natural resources, 6, 14
Nebraska, 5, 22, 25, 26
Oklahoma, 26, 29
plant, 6, 10, 13, 14
prairie, 6, 13, 14, 17, 26
regalia, 9
religious, 9, 13
reservation, 26, 29
river, 5, 6, 14
sacred, sacred bundles, 9, 10, 14
settlements, settlers, 5, 6, 25, 26

skin, 17, 18, 21
soldier, 22, 29
stampede, 18
star, 6, 9, 10, 13
sweat lodge, 10
tipi, 10, 13, 18, 21
tool, 9, 13, 17, 18, 21, 22
traded, trading, 14, 21, 22
Transcontinental Railroad, 25, 26
travel, 10, 18, 22, 25, 26
travois, 18
treaties, 22, 26
tribes, 5, 13, 14, 17, 18, 21, 22, 25, 29
United States, 25, 26, 29
village, 5, 9, 10, 13, 14, 17, 18, 29
war, warrior, 17, 21, 22, 25, 26, 29
weapon, 17, 26
woman, women, 9, 10, 13, 14, 18, 21, 29
work, worker, 13, 21, 25, 29

Editorial and Image Credits

Designer: Michael Sellner, Corporate Graphics, North Mankato, Minnesota
Consultant/Marketing Design: Alison Hagler, Basset and Becker Advertising, Columbus, Georgia

Images © copyright contributor unless otherwise specified.
Cover – "Skidi Pawnees" by W. Langdon Kihn. **4/5** – River: "Encampment Along the Platte" by Worthington Whittredge/Wikipedia; Aztecs: North Wind Picture Archives. **6/7** – Buffalo: Everett Collection Inc/Alamy; Indians: "Migrate with Dogs" by W. Langdon Kihn. **8/9** – Hand & World: Brandon Alms/iStockphoto; Stars: Clear View Images/iStockphoto; Bundle: Werner Forman/CORBIS. **10/11** – Village: "Skidi Pawnees" by W. Langdon Kihn; Earth Lodge: "Earth Lodge, Great Plains" by North Wind Picture Archives; Tipi: "Tipi" by Karl Bodmer/Wikipedia. **12/13** – Kurahu: "Rainmaking Among the Mandan" by George Catlin/Courtesy of Smithsonian American Art Museum; Water: "Water for Camp" by Charles Marion Russell/Wikipedia. **14/15** – Crops: NativeStock; Gatherers: North Wind Picture Archives. **16/17** – Warrior: North Wind Picture Archives; Fire: "Prairie Fire" by George Catlin. **18/19** – Horseback: George Catlin, National Archives of Canada, C-119982; Travois: "Migrate with Dogs" by W. Langdon Kihn; Wolf skins: "Hunting Buffalo Camouflaged with Wolf Skins" by George Catlin. **20/21** – Calumet: NativeStock; Two men: "Skidi Pawnees" by W. Langdon Kihn. **22/23** – Spaniards: "Coronado Making his Way Across New Mexico" by Frederic S. Remington; Travel group: "Plains People Moving Camp" by Charles Marion Russell. **24/25** – Wagon train: "Caravans Going West" by Alfred Jacob Miller; Battle: "The Silenced War Whoop" by Charles Schreyvoge/Wikipedia; Railroad: "The Last Spike" by Thomas Hill/Wikipedia. **26/27** – All: North Wind Picture Archives. **28/29** – Flag: Himasaram/Wikipedia; Indian affairs: Ken Blackbird, courtesy of Smithsonian National Museum of the American Indian, Washington DC (Pictured: Kevin Gover); Military group*: Toni Hill, Pawnee Nation of Oklahoma. *(Pictured left to right): 1SG Daniel Gilliss, B Co 1SG; Mr. Charles A. Lone Chief Jr., Pawnee Business Council (PBC) Vice-President; SPC Pearle Hare; Mr. Marshall Gover, Pawnee Nation President; LTC Paul Gass, 486th BN CDR; Mr. Richard Tilden, PBC Council Seat 1 Representative; CPT Thomas Rains B Co CDR. Picture taken at the Color Exchange of the 486th Battalion of the United States and Pawnee Nation.*

31

Think With Bagster

Use the information from the book to answer the questions below.

1. Pawnees used every part of the animals they hunted. They made cups from horns and shovels from shoulder blades. What other tools could they make from animal bones, hides, and flesh?

2. Pawnee women dug deep pits in the earth to store food. Why do you think they did this? How do you think they got into the pit when they needed food? How would they find what they needed in the dark pit?

3. In what ways did Pawnees help the United States grow? How did U.S. growth affect the Pawnee people?

4. Do you think Pawnee Indians should have agreed to give up their weapons and move to a reservation? How would this decision make you feel?

5. Write an article discussing the positive and negative impacts of the Transcontinental Railroad on life in the Great Plains and in other parts of America.